EXMOOR

A shortish guide

Robert Hesketh

Bossiney Books · Launceston

Other Bossiney books about Exmoor

Lynton and Lynmouth, a Shortish Guide
Shortish Walks on Exmoor (fifteen walks, 6-9 km)
Shortish Walks in north Devon
(fourteen walks, 6-8 km, four of them on Exmoor)

Pub Walks on Exmoor (ten walks, 8-15 km)

First published 2008 by Bossiney Books Ltd
Langore, Launceston, Cornwall PL15 8LD
www.bossineybooks.com
ISBN 978-1906474-00-3

Acknowledgements
The maps are by Graham Hallowell
The cover is based on a design by Heards Design Partnership
All photographs are by the author or from
the publishers' own collection

Printed in Great Britain by R Booth Ltd, Penryn, Cornwall

Introduction

High moorland and sea cliffs, rolling hills cut by fast flowing rivers and steep, wooded valleys, herds of red deer and its own breed of wild pony, Exmoor is endlessly enjoyable – provided you know where to go. This book is designed to help you find the best of Exmoor, its most beautiful and interesting places.

As well as features on Dunster, Porlock, Minehead and Lynton and Lynmouth, we suggest five drives, averaging only 40km (25 miles) but with ample to occupy a whole day. Also included are several short walks. Easy strolls which can be extended if you wish, they include some of Exmoor's most famous features – Tarr Steps, Badgeworthy Water, Heddon's Mouth and Watersmeet. Some other Bossiney books, listed opposite, include longer walks.

Robert Hesketh

Further information

Exmoor National Park Authority has four excellent centres, Dulverton 01398 323841, Combe Martin 01271 883319, Dunster (01643 821835) and Lynmouth (01548 763466). They are open daily 10-5, with interesting displays, helpful staff and a wide range of books and maps.

Also highly recommended are the Tourist Information Centres at Lynton (01598 752225) and Minehead (01643 702624). There are local information points at Withypool, Parracombe, Allerford, Brompton Regis, Wootton Courtenay, Wheddon Cross, Winsford, Challacombe, Barbrook, Simonsbath and Molland.

The Ordnance Survey Landranger 1:50,000 maps 180 and 181 cover Exmoor, west and east respectively. For more detail, and especially for walking, choose OL9 1:25,000, Exmoor, which is a double-sided sheet so very good value.

Exmoor ponies, well known in the West Country and beyond, are closer to the original wild stock than any other breed – images of their ancestors grace cave paintings in France and Spain. Like them, Exmoor ponies are strong and hardy, with thick coats to stand a northern climate and the ability to thrive on limited vegetation.

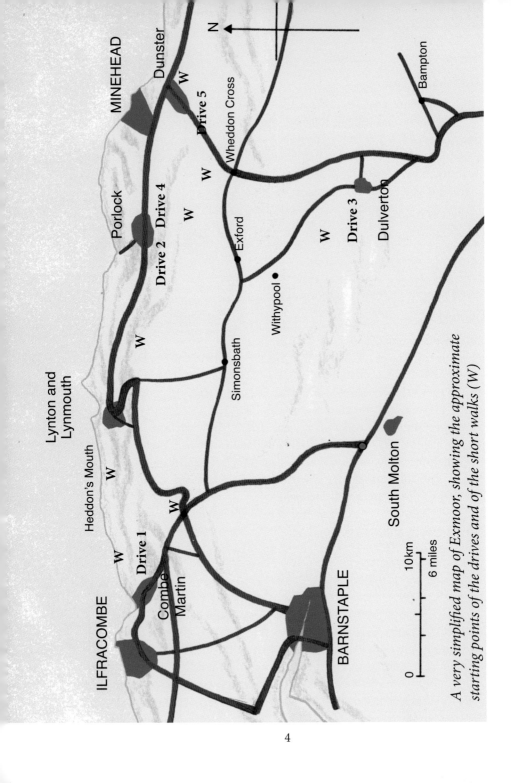

ILFRACOMBE

Lynton and Lynmouth

MINEHEAD

Dunster

Heddon's Mouth

W

W

W

Drive 1

Combe Martin

Porlock

W

Drive 2 Drive 4

W

W

Drive 5

W

Wheddon Cross

W

Simonsbath

Exford

Withypool

Drive 3

Dulverton

W

Bampton

N

BARNSTAPLE

South Molton

0

10km

6 miles

A very simplified map of Exmoor, showing the approximate starting points of the drives and of the short walks (W)

4

Exmoor's history

Exmoor's rugged topography and upland climate shaped its history, making it a place apart. It was occupied long before the Roman invasion, leaving a rich inheritance of stone circles and rows, ancient field systems and hillforts, although these are much less striking than those on Dartmoor.

Place names show Anglo-Saxon settlement in the sheltered valleys, but high Exmoor with thin soils and sparse grazing has few settlement names. The Norman kings made 80 km² (20,000 acres) out of Exmoor's 570 km² a Royal Forest, where hunting was reserved and poaching punished by harsh laws. Farmers had to pay the Crown for the right to graze animals. This established Exmoor's strong hunting tradition, helped maintain its wild character and further deterred settlement. Whilst the Normans built two wood and earth castles on Exmoor, Dunster Castle is the only major reminder of their military power.

Perhaps Exmoor's most impressive medieval structure is its most ancient bridge, Tarr Steps, a monument to the countless packhorse trains that carried goods to and from this remote region until wheeled vehicles arrived in the late 18th century. Exmoor's ports, including Minehead, earned a hard living from the sea and some settlements prospered from mining minerals, notably Combe Martin, but Exmoor as a whole remained a sparsely populated and underdeveloped area.

John Knight, a wealthy and energetic Midlands industrialist, bought the former Royal Forest in 1818. It contained one farm and a few ancient trackways, but Knight and his son Fredric set about transforming high Exmoor with new farms, houses, mines, a mineral railway and 35 km of roads. Enclosing fields with walls, shelterbelts and the beech hedges now characteristic of Exmoor, they ploughed the land to create permanent pasture – a massive undertaking.

Agriculture remains vital to Exmoor, tourism no less so. Tourism began during the Napoleonic Wars, when foreign travel was impossible and Romantics – including Wordsworth, Coleridge and Southey – extolled the abundant beauties of Exmoor's wild scenery. Lynton and Lynmouth were established as genteel resorts, as were Minehead and Combe Martin. First the railways and later the motor car made Exmoor accessible to far larger numbers of visitors. In recognition of Exmoor's great heritage of history, natural and man made, Exmoor became a National Park in 1954.

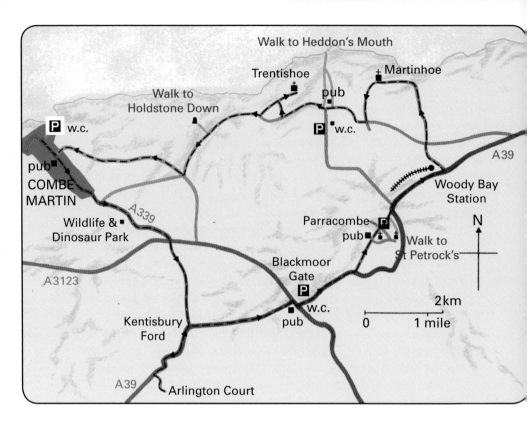

Drive 1   From Combe Martin

Distance: 41km (25 miles) (shorter if you omit Arlington Court)

Combe Martin, Kentisbury Ford, Arlington Court, Blackmoor Gate, Parracombe, Martinhoe Cross, Hunter's Inn, Trentishoe, Stony Corner, Combe Martin

From Combe Martin's sea front car park, turn left and drive up the main street, said to be the longest village street in England.

The unusual four-storey white building on the right after 1km is the unique Pack o' Cards, built by George Ley, the Squire of Combe Martin, in 1690. This remarkable inn – originally his home – fulfilled his promise to erect 'an everlasting monument to Lady Luck' after he won handsomely at cards. The Pack is inspired by a deck of 52 playing cards: 52 feet square, it has four storeys to represent the four suits. There are 52 windows and 52 steps in the staircase; 13 doors on each floor and 13 fireplaces. The four chimneys on the top floor represent the four kings and the four chimneys below the four queens.

Follow the street out of Combe Martin and uphill past the Wildlife and Dinosaur Park. Set in 10 hectares (25 acres) the park offers a variety of interest, including meerkats, a wolf pack and other animals, butterfly house, dinosaur shows, cinema, museum, a light show and 'the tomb of the pharaohs'.

Turn right (B3229), KENTISBURY FORD, BARNSTAPLE, ARLINGTON COURT – or simply drive straight on to Blackmoor Gate and follow the directions from there if you do not wish to visit Arlington Court.

Turn right BARNSTAPLE A39 ARLINGTON COURT at Kentisbury Ford. Take the second turning left, ARLINGTON COURT (brown sign).

Turn right out of Arlington Court car park and drive down to the A39. Turn right LYNTON A39. Drive on to a T-junction at Blackmoor Gate. Turn right and almost immediately left, LYNTON LYNMOUTH A39.

Continue for 1.5 km and turn left PARRACOMBE. Drive past the Fox and Goose, which has a collection of period photographs, including some of the horse-drawn Lynton/Barnstaple coach.

Parracombe has two churches. The older, St Petrock's, has a completely unspoilt Georgian interior, including box pews, a three deck pulpit and huge painted boards. If you wish to visit St Petrock's it is best to drive past the red telephone booth and leave your car in the signed car park just beyond Bodley Cross, then take a pleasant walk of around 750 m (1/2 mile) each way.

For this walk, turn right uphill out of the car park and after 150 m take the footpath on the right. This emerges by a bridge, spanning what was once the old railway. Turn left across the bridge.

Alternatively, you can drive up the narrow lane to St Petrock's, but parking is limited and drivers are obliged to turn around and retrace their route. Turn right at the telephone booth. Drive past the (relatively

---

Arlington Court is a fascinating house, with splendid grounds. Behind a modest Georgian façade there are tastefully furnished rooms packed with collections of model ships, paintings, shells, tapestries and pewter. There are vast stretches of parkland with flowers, mature specimen trees and rhododendrons.

The Victorian stables house a collection of over fifty carriages and harness. Regular horse harnessing demonstrations and carriage rides around the estate are provided in summer.

The narrow gauge Lynton & Barnstaple Railway, not completed until 1898, did much to popularise North Devon with visitors before its closure in 1935. It is now being lovingly restored

new) parish church into a cul-de-sac, CHURCH TOWN OLD CHURCH. Return to the telephone booth and turn right. Drive up to the A39.

Or, turn right out of the car park and continue to the A39. Turn left, LYNTON and take the second turning left, WOODY BAY STATION.

Now restored in Southern Railway style, complete with delightful period paraphernalia of art deco posters, red fire buckets and leather luggage, Woody Bay Station offers rides, usually steam-hauled, to a temporary station near Parracombe. Further extensions and restoration of the Lynton to Barnstaple line are planned for the future. Teas, light refreshments and railway souvenirs are on sale in the station.

Turn left out of the station. Take the next left, MARTINHOE WOODY BAY. Continue ahead at the crossroads. At a T-junction there is a parking area from which to enjoy the view towards Woody Bay.

Turn left MARTINHOE HUNTER'S INN. Follow the lane past Martinhoe's 11th century church, where the list of rectors goes back to 1270. Turn next right to Hunter's Inn and follow the lane steeply downhill. For the Heddon's Mouth walk (see page 10) or for the National Trust's information centre and shop which is renowned for its ice-cream, turn left and use the car park. There are public conveniences here too.

Turn left out of the car park and keep left, COMBE MARTIN (turn right at Hunter's Inn if not using the car park). To visit Trentishoe's charming church and enjoy some more wonderful views, take the second turning right – the first is 'unfit for motors'. Drive steeply uphill and turn right at the junction.

After visiting the church, begin to retrace your route, but do not turn left and downhill. Continue ahead to the next junction (Holdstone Down Cross) and join a slightly more major road.

Woody Bay, and beyond it the Valley of the Rocks, seen from a parking area five minutes drive beyond Woody Bay Station

The village of Parracombe, seen from near the old church, St Petrock's

The tiny church at Trentishoe, where the organ came from the SS Mauretania and the musician's gallery was too small for the double bass

Park at the sign HOLDSTONE DOWN 1146 FT VIEWPOINT. A gentle 500 m walk up to the summit is rewarded with panoramic views of the coast and rolling hills – and sometimes rolling fog, as seen in the photograph above!

Turn right at the next junction (Stony Corner), SILVER DALE NURSERY. This narrow lane gives a scenic return to Combe Martin. Turn right down the main street (King Street) and back to the start.

The Heddon's Mouth Walk

One of Exmoor's most attractive and popular short walks starts at Hunter's Inn and leads to the sea at Heddon's Mouth. A 3 km (2 mile) round trip on well-surfaced and mainly level paths, this walk has superb views of the towering cliffs and Heddon's Mouth Cleave. The Cleave (a Devon word for a deep, steep valley) is especially lovely in spring, with its wild flowers and in autumn, with its blazing colours.

From the National Trust car park, walk down the lane to Hunter's Inn. Turn left in front of the inn, COMBE MARTIN BARNSTAPLE. After 300 m, take the footpath right for HEDDON'S MOUTH. Ignore all side turnings and follow further signs for HEDDON'S MOUTH.

The path ends at the beach. Enjoy the view and then retrace your steps for 150 m. Cross the stream, then follow the path back up to Hunter's Inn.

Lynmouth

Lynmouth enjoys a superb natural setting where Exmoor meets the sea in a series of dramatic cliffs and steep wooded valleys. The Romantic poets were among early admirers. Shelley had a cottage here, whilst Robert Southey thought this one of the finest spots he ever saw.

Wild scenery can mean wild weather, as the Flood Memorial Hall with its evocative photographs from 1952 testifies. Just inside the Glen Lyn estate, noted for its waterfall, a sister lifeboat of the famous *Louisa* is on show. On a stormy January night in 1899, when launching from Lynmouth was impossible, *Louisa* was dragged by men and horses 22 km (14 miles) over Exmoor to Porlock. Launching from there, her crew shepherded the *Forrest Hall* and all aboard to safety.

Lynmouth is also noted for its pretty harbour and for the Rhenish Tower, a replica of the 19th century water tower destroyed in the 1952 flood (see page 16). However, the town's oldest building is The Rising Sun, which began as fishermen's cottages in the 14th century and became an inn approximately 500 years ago. It is said to have been used by smugglers (the fish-curing cellars provided convenient storage for contraband), as described in R D Blackmore's *Lorna Doone*.

A unique cliff railway joins Lynmouth and Lynton. Built in 1890, it is powered entirely by water, drawn off the West Lyn, and works by balancing the weight of its two cars on a pulley system. The top car's tank is filled with water, enabling it to descend and thus pull the lighter car from the bottom 261 m up the slope. When the first car reaches the bottom it dumps its load, 3000 litres of water. Brilliantly simple!

Before Lynton joined the main railway network in 1898, both villages were small settlements. The Rising Sun and parts of St Mary's in Lynton give an idea of what Lynton and Lynmouth looked like before the tourists came in force and late Victorian architecture, typified by Lynton's impressive town hall, began to dominate.

To see more of old Lynton, visit the museum. Housed in an 18th century cottage, it features agricultural and craftsmen's tools, period photographs, rocks and fossils. It has a good railway collection and pictures of the 1952 flood.

Scenery is Lynton's greatest asset. North Walk provides marvellous views of Exmoor's high cliffs and South Wales, and the dramatic Valley of Rocks (see photograph below), with its craggy tors and frost-riven features, is unique. Possibly these were the result of glacial action, exceptional in Devon, which mostly lay just south of the ice sheets that covered much of Britain during the last Ice Age. Now a dry valley, it once contained the Lyn river, which left considerable deposits of water-borne rocks.

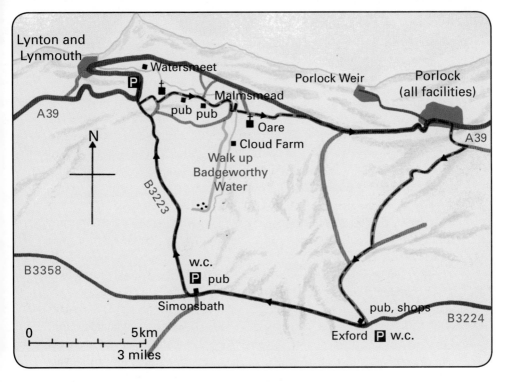

Drive 2   From Porlock onto the high moor

Distance: 56km (35 miles)   Can be linked to Drive 3 or Drive 4

Porlock, Hawkcombe, Exford, Simonsbath, Watersmeet, Rockford, Brendon, Malmsmead, Oare, Robber's Bridge, Porlock Hill, Porlock

This dramatically scenic route is definitely not to be hurried, especially as it uses some steep, very narrow lanes. Two beautiful riverside walks can be included, at Watersmeet – noted for its waterfalls and National Trust tearoom – and along the 'Doone Valley' from Malmsmead – the centre of RD Blackmore's Exmoor epic, *Lorna Doone*.

Turn right out of Porlock's Doverhay car park onto the main street and almost immediately right, DOVERHAY. Turn left when the lane divides, WEST LUCCOMBE. This lane climbs steeply through trees to a junction. Turn very sharp right and take the steep unsigned lane uphill.

It is worth stopping to enjoy the view of Porlock Bay when you reach the open moor. The lane dips and then climbs past Pool Farm.

Turn right at Porlock Post, EXFORD. There are more wonderful views from Stoke Pero Common. Follow the road down to Exford, which has a car park, tea rooms, hotels, shop, garage and toilets.

13

Porlock Bay, with the tide in and covering the salt marsh

Turn right, SIMONSBATH B3224. Exmoor's largest parish, Simonsbath, including its houses, church and school, was established in the mid 19th century by John Knight and his son, Fredric (see page 5).

Their agricultural 'improvements' also created Exmoor's patchwork landscape of green pastures and brown heather (purple in late summer). It takes imagination to picture Exmoor as it was before the Knights began their work – but the next part of this drive with its great vistas of 'unimproved' moorland more than 400 m above sea level helps.

Follow the road on through Simonsbath and around to the right, LYNTON. Emerging onto wide open moor, the road climbs to the Devon border at Brendon Two Gates before descending to the A39 at Hillsford Bridge.

On the way it crosses the infant river Exe, 1 km east of Exe Head. At this point, the start of its long journey via Tiverton and Exeter to the sea at Exmouth, Exmoor's greatest river is only a stream. Like the West Lyn, the Barle and Hoaroak Water, the Exe rises on the edge of the Chains, Exmoor's watershed. Here, at a height of between 450 m and 480 m, rainfall averages over 1780 mm (nearly six feet) per year.

Drainage is limited because of the geology – an impermeable iron pan lies very near or on the surface. Whilst the West Lyn and Hoaroak Water flow north, the rivers Exe and Barle flow south and east through deepening valleys to their confluence just south of Dulverton.

Turn right, LYNMOUTH PORLOCK A39. Park at the pay and display under a rock face and walk down the footpath to Watersmeet, where the East and West Lyn join in a deep gorge. (See page 16.)

After your visit to Watersmeet, retrace your route to Hillsford Bridge. Turn left SIMONSBATH and almost immediately left again up a steep, unsigned lane, which includes a dramatic view of the Lyn gorges. Turn left at the next junction, ROCKFORD BRENDON OARE. Rockford and Brendon both have attractive inns by the river, and the Rockford Inn brews its own beer. Stop at the Lorna Doone Farm car park (toilets, refreshments). This is the probable site of Jan Ridd's home, 'Plover's Barrow Farm' in the novel. (See page 17 for a walk.)

From the Lorna Doone car park, cross the bridge and continue to Oare church, where Lorna was shot on her wedding day by the villainous Carver Doone. (Fear not, it was a Victorian novel and she recovered to live happily ever after with Jan!)

Continue straight ahead at Oare church, where the lane gets even narrower. Drive on over Robber's Bridge. With the aid of a couple of hairpins, the lane rises to the A39. Turn right and follow the beautiful coast road towards Porlock Hill and one of Exmoor's greatest viewpoints, with a long stretch of the Welsh coast ahead and Exmoor's highest point, Dunkery Beacon (519m), behind.

Below, under the heathery flank of Bossington Hill, is Porlock Bay with its pebble ridge almost in plan view. Formed 8000 years ago by rising sea levels, this ridge was breached in 1996 and subsequent storms have moved the beach 20-30m inland, cutting a canyon through the marsh clay that can be plainly seen from this high vantage point. The encroaching sea has turned what was freshwater marsh into tidal salt marsh, often visited by estuarine birds including shelduck, oyster catcher, gulls and curlew.

Descend Porlock Hill in low gear to return to the start of the drive. In the early days of motor racing, climbing Porlock Hill with its 25% gradient and sharp bends was taken as a major challenge for the most robust cars. Motor engineering has advanced greatly, but Porlock Hill remains the same. (For Porlock itself, see page 22.)

15

With its deep wooded gorges and waterfalls, Watersmeet is impressive at any season, not least in Winter with the rivers in spate, and in Autumn, when the trees are a blaze of colour

Watersmeet

This scene with its rushing waters is always dramatic, especially after heavy rain. However, no one would wish for another flood like that of August 1952. Over 225mm (9 inches) of rain had fallen on Exmoor in just two days. Spates swept down the East and West Lyn, powered by more water than flows down the Thames in three months. Destroying houses and taking cars far out to sea, the flood killed 34 people.

Cross a footbridge and, if you wish, divert right for 400m, up steps, WATERFALL VIEWPOINT. Retrace your steps to the footbridge. Cross a second bridge to the National Trust's shop cum information centre and tea room – formerly a shooting and fishing lodge.

The approach to Malmsmead from Brendon takes you through the valley of the East Lyn River. On one side of the valley is thick woodland, the other side a scree slope

The ford and bridge at Lorna Doone Farm, seen here in late Spring

The Doone Valley walk

If you would like an attractive literary walk, take LANE LEADING TO PUBLIC FOOTPATH DOONE VALLEY (or pay 50p and use the riverbank path). After 250 m, bear left, BRIDLEWAY DOONE VALLEY. At Cloud Farm (teas and lunches) continue ahead, BRIDLEWAY DOONE VALLEY.

The walk can be continued on this lovely bankside path by Badgeworthy Water for 2.5 km to see the Doone's lair, at a point where the main path takes a right turn away from the river. In real life, it is an abandoned medieval village, containing ruins typical of local longhouses, with one room for the farmer's family and one for the animals. It has decayed greatly since Blackmore wrote *Lorna Doone* in 1869 – you need imagination to see the robber Doone clan in all their wicked splendour, especially when the bracken is high. Return to the car park.

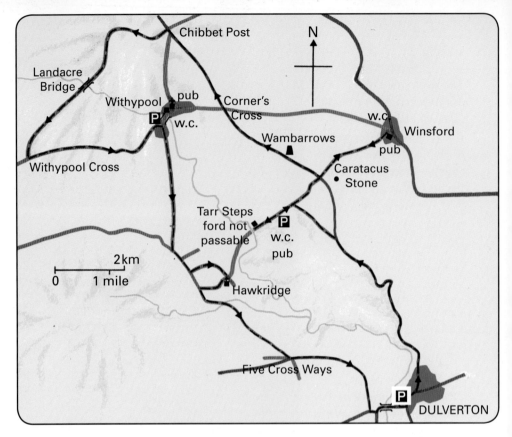

Drive 3 From Dulverton to Tarr Steps and Withypool

Distance: 50km (31 miles)

Dulverton, Mounsey Hill Gate, Tarr Steps, Winsford, Winsford Hill, Chibbet Post, Landacre Bridge, Withypool, Hawkridge, Dulverton

Can be linked with Drive 2, by turning right at Chibbet Post down into Exford

This exploration of the southern moor is packed with interest and affords magnificent views of open moorland and river valleys. The bridges are of special interest: medieval Tarr Steps is one of England's finest and longest clapper bridges. Also in the route are Exmoor's oldest arched bridge, Landacre, two further handsome arched bridges at Dulverton and Withypool and seven bridges at Winsford.

Leave your car in the main Dulverton car park to visit the Exmoor National Park Centre in the town square. This is open all year with helpful staff and a good range of books, maps and videos. In the same

Tarr Steps and the riverside walk

Tarr Steps is a clapper bridge 36m long, constructed from 17 slabs of flat stone, each weighing two tonnes and over 2m long.

Nonetheless, the force of water generated by the 1952 flood was so great that most of Tarr Steps was washed downriver. Fortunately, it had already been carefully surveyed and engineers knew exactly where to put the recovered stones. Whilst the ford adjacent to Tarr Steps may have been used as part of a prehistoric trackway, most authorities agree the bridge itself is medieval.

On the left of Tarr Steps is 16th century Tarr Farm, now an inn and restaurant providing refreshments all year. Many pleasant walks are possible from Tarr Steps. The simplest is to follow the well beaten path upriver on the eastern bank as far as you wish – the Royal Oak at Withypool is a pleasant 5km each way.

building is the Heritage Centre (open Easter to October), an excellent museum of Exmoor life.

Drive left out of the car park and keep left, EXFORD LYNTON, into the square. Turn left, B3223 LYNTON TARR STEPS EXFORD. This attractive road leads alongside the river Barle, and then uphill through the woods onto open moor. Cross a cattle grid and turn left, TARR STEPS. Turn next left, TARR STEPS. Leave your car in the car park and follow the path downhill to Tarr Steps (500m).

The Exmoor wool trade was sufficient to maintain Winsford's 'Royal Oak' and largely pay for the 15th century church rebuilding, including the impressive 27m tall church tower

From the Tarr Steps car park, turn right and drive uphill. Keep left at Liscombe Farm, WINSFORD. Cross the B3223 at Spire Cross. Stop at the first parking area on the right and walk 100m to a stone shelter to see the 'Caratacus Stone', a rare 5th or 6th century relic. Inscribed CARACCI NEPUS, it probably commemorates a descendant or kinsman of Caratacus, the Silurian king who fought the Roman invaders.

Drive downhill to Winsford, one of Somerset's prettiest villages, and leave your car in the car park by the tea rooms. Before the arrival of turnpike roads and wheeled vehicles in the early 19th century, Winsford's seven small bridges carried packhorses laden with Exmoor wool.

Retrace your route to Spire Cross. Turn right EXFORD WITHYPOOL. Drive on for only 1.3km (³/4 mile) to the top of Winsford Hill. At 426m the triangulation pillar on Winsford Hill is the highest point on the drive. Beside it stand the Bronze Age burial chambers of Wambarrows. All have been despoiled and are said to be haunted. The view, covering a great swathe of Exmoor including Dunkery to the north and Dartmoor to the south, is highly memorable.

That Winsford Hill is so well preserved is largely thanks to the Acland family, who leased it to the National Trust in 1918. Sir Thomas Dyke Acland ensured the survival of the Exmoor pony as a distinct breed by establishing a breeding herd here in the mid 19th century. (Please do not feed the ponies – it encourages them to wander into danger on the roads and to take unsuitable foods.)

Drive on for 5km past Corner's Cross to Chibbet Post. Turn left, LANDACRE NORTH MOLTON. Slow down for the ford and continue

to Landacre Bridge (see photograph above), a popular picnic spot. Considered Exmoor's oldest arched bridge, Landacre was repaired as early as 1621 so was probably built well before that date.

Continue to Withypool Cross. Turn sharp left, WITHYPOOL. Enjoy the views on the way down to the village. To explore the village, turn left and leave your car in the signed car park on the left. Walk across the bridge (1866), past the post office/information point, noting the tea room opposite, with its vintage petrol pumps, and The Royal Oak, an inn of traditional character. From 1927-1935, the landlord was Charles Maxwell Knight who led a double life. He was the spy-master on whom Ian Fleming (who worked for him) modelled the character M in his James Bond stories.

Turn right out of the Withypool car park. Keep ahead, HAWKRIDGE at Withypool Post. Turn left at a slanting T-junction, then take the second left. (Several signs were damaged or missing when we last drove this route, but it should say HAWKRIDGE.)

Arriving in Hawkridge, turn right, DULVERTON. You may want to stop to visit St Giles church, which is mainly fourteenth and fifteenth century, with a Norman font and south doorway. Note too the stone coffin lid, inscribed in Norman French rather than the then prevailing Latin. Take the next turning left (Colland Cross) for DULVERTON. Follow the series of DULVERTON signs back to the start.

Porlock

Said to date from 1290, Porlock's Ship Inn (above) is known locally as 'the Top Ship' to distinguish it from the equally charming 'Bottom Ship' at Porlock Weir. A Grade II listed building, it is one of England's oldest inns and has a thatched roof, exposed beams, a gothic window and huge open fireplaces. 'Southey's Corner' is in the chimneystack and honours Poet Laureate Robert Southey who wrote a sonnet here in 1798, celebrating Porlock.

Licensees of the inn have been traced to 1744, when most travellers arrived on foot or horseback. With the coming of turnpike roads and stagecoaches, stabling was developed at the Ship, which provided two extra horses to drag coaches up the notoriously steep Porlock Hill.

Porlock's church is dedicated to the 7th century Welsh Saint Dubricius, who is said to have crowned King Arthur. Its most striking feature is its wood shingle spire. Inside is a particularly impressive piece of medieval sculpture: John, 4th Lord Harrington (died 1418) is carved in alabaster, wearing full armour as he did when he fought for Henry V at the Battle of Agincourt. Beside him lies his wife, Elizabeth Courtenay – her costume is also intricately carved. In the west wall are two small fragments of a Saxon Cross shaft – the earliest Christian relics in West Somerset.

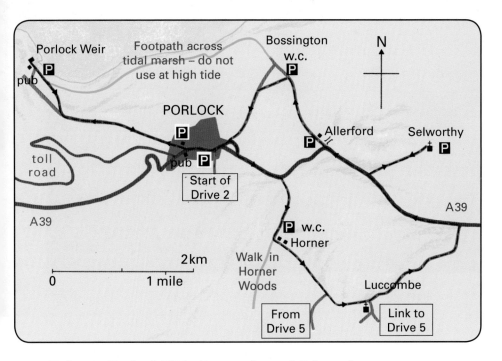

Drive 4 Porlock Weir, Luccombe and Selworthy

Distance: 20km (12 miles)

Porlock, Porlock Weir, Horner, Luccombe, Selworthy, Allerford, Bossington and Porlock

Can be linked to Drive 5 at Luccombe or Drive 2 at the start

This delightful route includes some of Exmoor's most attractive villages. Each has a range of vernacular buildings in cob or stone, roofed with traditional thatch or pantiles. Many have the characteristically West Country lateral chimneystacks – set in the side wall rather than an end wall, and often with bread ovens built into them. It is worth taking time to explore these villages on foot and also to enjoy a gentle woodland walk at Horner.

From the Doverhay car park at Porlock, turn left and drive down the main street. Turn right WEST END for PORLOCK WEIR. Leave your car at Porlock Weir car park. Enjoy the views of the pretty harbour and the bay and refreshments at the 16th century Ship. Part thatched and built of beach stone with lime mortar, the Ship has exposed beams (some are ship's timbers), period photos and lateral chimneystacks.

Retrace your route to Porlock. Turn left down the main street. Continue ahead, MINEHEAD A39. Turn right, HORNER LUCCOMBE. Stop at Horner car park for a gentle walk in the woods.

Continuing from Horner car park, keep ahead at the next crossroads LUCCOMBE. The beautiful church here is surrounded by limewashed buildings in the Somerset vernacular (see cover photograph).

Turn your car around. Take the first turning right, MINEHEAD. Follow the lane around to the left at the next cross, MINEHEAD. Turn left at the A39 junction, PORLOCK WEST LUCCOMBE. Take the first right, SELWORTHY. Continue past the medieval tithe barn to the car park opposite the church and explore the village on foot (see page 26).

A walk in Horner Woods

This huge area of ancient woodland (330 hectares or 800 acres) is rich in wildlife, especially mosses, lichen and fungi, though it is also noted for its birds and wildflowers. A pleasant, near level walk begins from the information board, turning right past the tearooms and then turning left for HORNER WOODS. Follow the broad track ahead, over the bridge and upstream, keeping Horner Water on your left. This can be extended for 3km (2 miles), ignoring side turnings, or for many miles more if you have an Ordnance Survey map and are ready for steep slopes.

Opposite:
Porlock Weir

Right, top:
The pack-
horse bridge
at Allerford,
a reminder
of transport
on Exmoor
when trains of
laden horses
carried goods.
Wheeled
vehicles only
became
common in
the 19th
century

Right, lower:
Cottages at
Bossington

From Selworthy, retrace your route to the A39 and turn right. Turn third right, ALLERFORD BOSSINGTON. You might want to stop at Allerford's small car park to visit the Rural Life Museum opposite. Housed in a 19th century school, it has three rooms of exhibits, showing local life on the farm, in the workshop and at home. A fourth room houses the West Somerset Photographic Archive.

On the right of the museum is a much photographed 17th century packhorse bridge.

Continue ahead into Bossington. Leave your car in the car park and explore this exceptionally attractive village on foot. Turn your car right out of the car park and first left PORLOCK. Turn right and right again to return to the start.

Selworthy

Selworthy is one of Somerset's most beautiful villages. Its thatched, limewashed cottages, including the charming tea rooms, surround the village green in an English idyll. Indeed, Selworthy was rebuilt in 1828 by Sir Thomas Acland of Killerton, Devon. A philanthropist, Sir Thomas designed the 'model' village himself, using traditional building materials to provide housing for the aged and infirm retainers of his Holnicote Estate. Holnicote's 12,443 acres are now the National Trust's main property on Exmoor. The Trust also cares for Selworthy and runs the shop and information centre.

All Saints church at the top of the village enjoys a remarkably beautiful position, overlooking the highest and wildest scenery of Exmoor, including Dunkery Beacon. The Perpendicular church, surprisingly lavish for a small community, is brilliant white, periodically coated with a traditional protective mix of lime and tallow.

Its greatest treasure is the south aisle and its glorious wagon roof, dating from the 1530s. Take time to look at the bosses (binoculars will help). Large windows and slim piers make Selworthy an exceptionally light and airy church. The late medieval pulpit retains its 17th century hourglass and sounding board, by which the lengthy and no doubt sonorous sermons of the day were measured and amplified before wristwatches and microphones. The splendid gallery is 18th century. Here, the church musicians played with the congregation facing them before the organ displaced them in 1879.

Minehead

The fact that there is an old Minehead may come as a surprise to many visitors. It is tucked away in Higher Town around the church, and also around the harbour. Quay Road has a number of 17th and 18th century buildings, reflecting Minehead's past sea trade. 'The best port and safest harbour in Somerset', was Daniel Defoe's judgement on Minehead. Its trade was with Virginia and the West Indies, but chiefly Ireland, especially in coarse wool for Taunton's sergemakers. Minehead's town arms aptly show a ship and a woolpack. When Taunton's cloth trade declined during the 18th century, Minehead suffered badly.

But the new fashion for English seaside holidays, promoted by the Hanoverian kings, revived Minehead's fortunes. The tide began to turn for Minehead during the Napoleonic Wars when Continental travel was impossible. The town then grew greatly as a tourist resort in both the 19th and 20th centuries. Butlin's holiday camp, looking like a vast wigwam, is a prominent part of the bay.

To see Higher Town with its stone and thatched cottages and historic church, park near the sculpture on Quay Road and take the footpath NORTH HILL, ST MICHAEL'S CHURCH, CHURCH STEPS. St Michael's is an impressive hillside church with a 26m tall tower, where a light for ships was kept. The church's greatest treasures are an illuminated missal of 1320, a carved font (1400) and a fine wooden screen.

From Minehead's station, the West Somerset Railway's passenger trains steam eastwards along the coast and then south to Bishop's Lydeard. Like all the stations along this attractive 32km (20 mile) route, Minehead has been restored in period Great Western style.

A walk round Dunster

Turn left out of Dunster Steep car park, near the excellent Information Centre. Continue up to the main street, then down past the medieval Luttrell Arms. Once the Abbot of Cleve's house, this imposing building is named after the powerful Luttrell family, who came into possession of Dunster Castle in 1376 and owned it until 1976.

The polygonal yarn market recalls the town's once thriving cloth trade. First built by George Luttrell around 1589, it has a central stone core supporting a lean-to roof with strong beams and dormers.

The main street turns sharp right. Walk ahead to the castle (National Trust, seasonal opening, 01643 821314). Dramatically sited, it began as a Norman motte-and-bailey castle. Hike to the top of the beautiful terraced garden to appreciate the military qualities of this superb hilltop site and the panoramic views. Of the later medieval castle, only the gatehouse remains, but it must have been strong to hold out against several months' siege during the Civil War.

What we see now is the 17th century mansion, handsomely remodelled by Anthony Salvin in 1868-72 for the Luttrell family. Packed with interest, its most notable features include plasterwork ceilings, a large collection of portrait paintings and the wonderfully baroque oak staircase. Leave by way of the gardens with their palms and national collection of strawberry trees.

Opposite: The Yarn Market

Right, top: Gallox Bridge was built just wide enough for trains of packhorses to cross – the parapets were kept low to allow the horses to cross easily with their wide loads, carried on panniers

Right, lower: The medieval dovecote, which supplied the monks with fresh meat

After visiting the castle, turn left at the shop. Walk down the lane and turn left into WEST STREET and left again, WATER MILL. Follow the mill leat down to the sign PACKHORSE BRIDGE. Walk ahead if you wish to visit the 18th century mill, fully restored and now milling flour that can be bought on site. Otherwise, turn right and then left past thatched cottages to the medieval Gallox Bridge.

Retrace your steps to West Street. Although it does not look especially old at first glance, the Stag's Head is one of Exmoor's most intriguing inns. A listed medieval building whose features include stone hearths,

The priory church's 30 metre tall red sandstone tower dates from 1443. Inside, its beautiful 15th century rood screen is the most striking of its many features. At 16.5 m, it is possibly the longest in England. There are also medieval monuments and iron-bound chests and an 18th century brass chandelier. The Royal Coat of Arms, 1660, reminds visitors of how bravely Dunster was defended during the long Civil War siege

exposed beams and masonry, it began as an open hall house about 1400, the smoke from open fires simply percolating upwards and out through the roof.

Continue up West Street to visit the church. Leave through the north door to see the medieval barn and dovecote. This supplied the monks with fresh meat and eggs and retains its 400 year old revolving ladder in full working order.

Retrace your steps through the church and turn left into Church Street (beware of the traffic). On the left is the Nunnery, a three-storey 14th century house. The overhanging upper storeys are slate-hung. Continue up the main street past the yarn market and the Luttrell Arms to the car park.

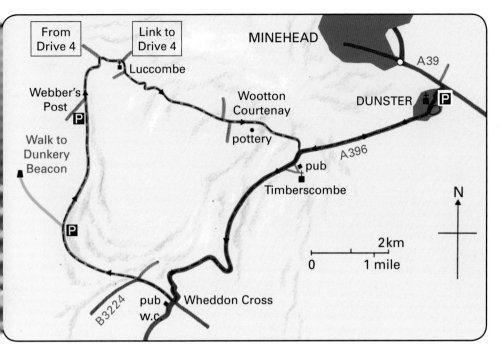

Drive 5   From Dunster to Dunkery and Luccombe

Distance: 32km (20 miles)   Can be linked to Drive 4 at Luccombe

Minehead, Dunster, Timberscombe, Wheddon Cross, Dunkery,
Webber's Post, Wooton Courtenay, Dunster, Minehead

This drive combines magnificent scenery, including the highest point
on Exmoor – Dunkery Beacon – with the historic interest of Dunster.

From Dunster, drive south up the A396 towards Wheddon Cross. The
road skirts Timberscombe, an attractive red sandstone village with a
pleasing church and pub. It is worth a diversion.

Turn right at Wheddon Cross, EXFORD AND DUNKERY BEACON. At
the next junction, where the main road veers left, continue ahead,
DUNKERY BEACON LUCCOMBE.

Leave your car at Dunkery Gate parking area (by the cattle grid)
and take the clear, well beaten path to the top of Dunkery. This mod-
erate ascent is rewarded with panoramic views of northern Exmoor,
far along the Bristol Channel and over the sea to Wales.

Return to your car and continue on the same road. Drive slowly
to enjoy the superb view of Porlock Bay as you descend Luccombe
Hill. (There are pleasant views from the car park at Webber's Post.)

The start of the walk up to Dunkery Beacon

Continue down to a T-junction. Turn right for LUCCOMBE, where the church is well worth stopping to see. Continue on the same lane, following the WOOTTON COURTENAY signs.

Visitors are welcome at the Mill Pottery, signed at the far end of Wootton Courtenay. Michael Gaitskell always has an interesting range of his distinctive hand-crafted stoneware on view. Distinguished by bold geometric designs, striking glazes and generously rounded forms, each pot has its own character. Much of the power for the pottery is provided by the restored mill wheel, linked to a generator.

Continue to the A396. Turn left, DUNSTER.

Michael Gaitskell, potter in Wootton Courtenay